Things you should already know,

but probably don't.

Useful knowledge for day to day life

Table of Contents

Table of Contents Cont.

Introduction

We live in a world filled with countless little mysteries—things we encounter every day but rarely stop to question. From the numbers on your toaster dial to why your alarm always seems to go off when you're in the deepest sleep, there's a fascinating world of simple, overlooked details all around us.

This book is a collection of those everyday curiosities, the things you probably interact with but never really thought about. Why does a clock run clockwise? What's the real reason we say "bless you" when someone sneezes? And have you ever wondered why the "close door" button on the elevator seems to mock you by never working?

Each of these everyday "mysteries" has a backstory, a scientific explanation, or sometimes even an odd quirk of history behind it. And once you know them, you'll not only be armed with useful knowledge for day-to-day life, but you'll also start seeing the world through a new lens of curiosity and wonder.

So flip through, explore these little-known facts, and get ready to be surprised by the simple things you probably should already know—but maybe don't.

How to Tell If the Moon is Waxing or Waning

It's easy to look up at the moon and wonder whether it's waxing (growing) or waning (shrinking), especially if you don't keep track of its phases every night. But there's a simple trick to help you tell which phase it's in just by looking at its shape.

WAXING: GROWING BIGGER

When the moon is waxing, it means the illuminated part of the moon

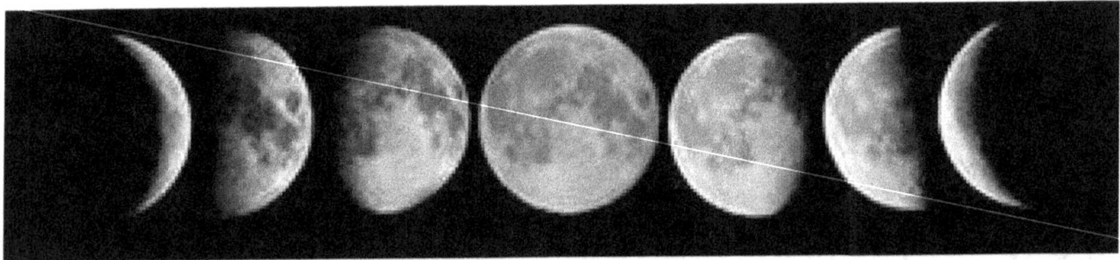

is getting bigger each night. Here's an easy way to remember it:
If the moon looks like a D (with the curved part on the right), it's developing—meaning it's waxing. Over the next several days, you'll see more and more of the moon's surface lit up until it becomes a full moon.

WANING: GETTING SMALLER

When the moon is waning, it's shrinking or losing light each night. If the moon looks like a C (with the curved part on the left), think of it as closing—the illuminated part is getting smaller, and it's on its way to becoming a new moon, where the moon will be fully in shadow.

This visual trick works especially well in the Northern Hemisphere. You can also remember that a waxing moon rises in the afternoon and is visible in the evening, while a waning moon rises later in the night and is more likely to be visible in the early morning.

THE CYCLE

The entire moon cycle from new moon to full moon and back again takes about 29.5

days, so the waxing and waning phases happen fairly quickly. Keeping this little trick in mind makes it easy to look up at the sky and know at a glance which direction the moon is headed in its cycle.

Vehicle Dashboard Symbols: What They Mean and How to Use Them

Most people glance at their vehicle's dashboard daily, but many might not realize just how much information those little symbols are trying to convey. Understanding these symbols can help you avoid issues and save you time, especially when you're driving a vehicle other than your own.

THE GAS TANK SYMBOL: WHICH SIDE IS IT ON?

One of the most useful, yet overlooked, features of your dashboard is the gas tank symbol. Most vehicles—whether cars, trucks, or other vehicles—display a small gas pump icon near the fuel gauge. Next to this icon, you'll often see a small arrow or triangle pointing either to the left or the right. This arrow tells you which side of the vehicle the fuel cap is on.

So, if you're borrowing or driving a new vehicle and don't know which side to pull up to at the gas station, just glance at this arrow. If it points to the right, the fuel cap is on the passenger side; if it points to the left, it's on the driver's side.

CHECK ENGINE LIGHT

The check engine light can be one of the most intimidating symbols. It's often a picture of an engine or a warning light that says "check engine." This light can mean a wide range of issues, from something as simple as a loose gas cap to more serious problems like engine misfires or transmission issues. The best course of action is to have it checked with a diagnostic tool if you're unsure.

BATTERY WARNING LIGHT

This symbol looks like a small battery, and when it lights up, it usually means your vehicle's charging system isn't working properly. It could be an issue with the battery, alternator, or wiring, and it's a good idea to check it out before the vehicle stops working altogether.

Why Do Soda Cans Have Two Different Openings?

At first glance, the tab on a soda can might seem pretty simple—its main job is to help you pop the top open and enjoy your drink. But there's actually a handy little trick that most people don't notice. Once you've opened your soda, you can flip the tab around, and it's designed to hold your straw in place!

THE STRAW HOLDER YOU NEVER KNEW

The hole in the middle of the can tab isn't just a design feature—it's

there to keep your straw from floating around or tipping out of the can. After you open your soda, simply spin the tab around so the hole lines up with the opening of the can. When you place your straw through the hole, it'll stay secure, making it easier to drink without the straw floating up or splashing out.

This little feature is especially useful if you're sipping while driving or trying to avoid spills, but it's something most people overlook, even though it's been a part of soda can designs for years!

WHY NOT JUST DRINK FROM THE CAN?

If you prefer drinking straight from the can, you're not alone. But some people like using a straw, especially for carbonated drinks, as it helps reduce contact with the acidity of the soda on their teeth. Using the tab as a straw holder is just an extra bonus feature for those who like a little more control over their sipping.

Why Are Interstate Highways Numbered the Way They Are?

The numbering system for U.S. interstate highways isn't random—it's actually designed to be very logical and easy to follow once you understand the rules. Created by the American Association of State Highway Officials in the nineteen fifties, the system has some basic principles that make it consistent across the country.

EVEN AND ODD NUMBERS

Interstate highways with even numbers (such as I-10, I-40, or I-90) run east-west. The numbers get higher as you move from the southern states up to the northern ones. For example, I-10 is far down south, while I-90 is much farther north.

Meanwhile, interstates with odd numbers (such as I-5, I-35, or I-95) run north-south. These numbers increase from the west to the east. So, I-5 runs along the West Coast, while I-95 follows the East Coast.

THREE-DIGIT INTERSTATES

When you see an interstate with a three-digit number (like I-495 or I-275), it's usually a spinoff or loop of a major interstate. These interstates connect to their two-digit "parent" highways. For example, I-495 is a loop that branches off from I-95 around Washington, D.C.

If the first digit of a three-digit interstate is even, it forms a loop around a city. If the first digit is odd, it's a spur that shoots out from a main highway and typically connects to a city center.

MILE MARKERS AND EXIT NUMBERS

Many states also use the interstate highway mile markers to number their exits. This means the exit numbers correspond with how many miles you've traveled on that highway. It makes navigation easier, as you can estimate how far the next exit is just by looking at the mile markers.

The Origins

The numbering system for interstates mirrors, in many ways, the U.S. Highway System (the pre-interstate system, such as Route 66). That older system had a similar odd-and-even numbering setup but wasn't as consistent in how it was applied across the country.

This numbering system helps people plan trips, find routes, and navigate across the country. It's a great example of a well-thought-out system that often goes unnoticed by everyday drivers but is essential for our transportation infrastructure.

How to Find North Using an Analog Watch

When you're out in the wilderness or even in the middle of a city and need to figure out which way is north, but you don't have a compass, your analog watch can be a handy tool. It's a simple trick that works when the sun is shining, and here's how to do it:

FINDING NORTH IN THE NORTHERN HEMISPHERE

If you're in the Northern Hemisphere, follow these steps:

1. Hold your watch flat and point the hour hand (the smaller hand) at the sun.

2. Once the hour hand is lined up with the sun, find the midpoint between the hour hand and 12 o'clock on your watch. 

3. That midpoint is pointing south, so if you're facing that direction, north will be directly behind you.

For example, if it's 4:00 p.m., you would point the hour hand at the sun, and the midpoint between 4 and 12 (which is 2) would be pointing south.

WHAT ABOUT THE SOUTHERN HEMISPHERE?

In the Southern Hemisphere, the method is slightly different. Instead of using the hour hand, you use 12 o'clock on your watch. Point 12 at the sun, and then the midpoint between 12 and the hour hand will point north.

WHY IT WORKS

This trick works because the sun is always in the southern part of the sky in the Northern Hemisphere, and in the northern part in the Southern Hemisphere. The watch's hour hand helps align you with the sun's position relative to the earth's rotation.

A FEW THINGS TO KEEP IN MIND

- → •This method only works during daylight hours, and the farther you are from the equator, the more accurate it is.
- → •If you're using a digital watch, just imagine where the hour hand would be at that time and follow the same steps.

What Causes the Smell After Rain?

You've probably noticed that distinct, earthy smell that fills the air after a rainstorm. That refreshing scent has a name—petrichor—and it's more than just a pleasant odor; it's the result of a few natural processes at play.

THE SCIENCE BEHIND PETRICHOR

Petrichor is mainly caused by a compound called geosmin, which is produced by soil-dwelling bacteria known as actinomycetes. When the rain hits the ground, especially after a dry spell, it causes geosmin to be released into the air, creating that recognizable earthy smell.

Geosmin is incredibly sensitive to the human nose, which is why even a small amount of rain can trigger this scent. Interestingly, this compound is so strong that we can detect it in concentrations as low as five parts per trillion!

OZONE AND RAINFALL

Another contributor to the post-rain smell is ozone, especially during thunderstorms. When lightning strikes, it splits nitrogen and oxygen molecules in the atmosphere, which can form ozone. Winds carry this ozone closer to the ground, and it adds a slightly sharp, fresh note to the earthy petrichor scent.

PLANT OILS

There's also another factor in the mix. Plants and trees release certain oils during dry periods, which build up on surfaces like rocks and soil. When rain hits these surfaces, the oils are flushed out into the air, adding another layer to the scent of petrichor.

Why Does the Rearview Mirror Flip?

That little tab on your rearview mirror is more useful than many people realize. It's designed to help reduce the glare from headlights behind you when you're driving at night. But how does it work?

THE DAY/NIGHT TOGGLE

The mirror in most vehicles has a day/night mode that is controlled by a small tab or lever at the bottom of the mirror. During the day, the mirror reflects a full image of the road behind you. But at night, bright headlights from vehicles behind can create dangerous glare, making it harder to see.

Flipping the tab adjusts the mirror's angle so that only a small amount of light is reflected toward your eyes. This creates a dimmer reflection of the road behind, making it easier to see without being blinded by headlights.

HOW IT WORKS

Rearview mirrors are made from prismatic glass, which means they have a wedge-like shape. The thicker side of the wedge reflects the full image during the day, while flipping the tab at night changes the angle so that light is reflected from the thinner edge. This causes the image to dim, reducing the glare but still allowing you to see the outline of cars behind you.

WHEN TO USE IT

The day/night feature is particularly helpful during nighttime driving when headlights from behind can be distracting or dangerous. By dimming the reflection, it helps reduce eye strain and improves your visibility of the road ahead.

How to Turn Off the Sound on a Microwave Oven

Microwaves are convenient, but the beeping they make—especially late at night or early in the morning—can be annoying. Luckily, most modern microwave ovens have a way to turn off the sound, though it's not always obvious.

THE MUTE OPTION

Many microwave ovens come with a mute function that allows you to turn off the sound. This feature is often called a "silent mode" or simply "sound off." Here's how to do it on most models:

1. Look for a dedicated mute button: Some microwave ovens have a button on the control panel labeled "Sound," "Mute," or something similar. Pressing it will toggle the beeps on or off.

2. Use a key combination: If your microwave doesn't have a visible mute button, you might be able to mute the beeping by pressing a specific combination of buttons. On many models, holding down the number "2" or "0" for about three seconds will mute the sound. Check your microwave's manual for the exact instructions.

3. Check the settings menu: Some advanced models have a settings menu you can access through the display. Navigate to the sound settings and switch the beeping off.

4. Reset if needed: If you ever want to turn the sound back on, you can repeat the same steps to unmute your microwave.

WHY IT'S USEFUL

Turning off the sound can be especially useful if you live in a shared space or don't want to wake someone up with the loud beeps that signal the end of cooking. Whether you're sneaking a late-night snack or just trying to keep the kitchen noise down, knowing how to mute your microwave can make things a little quieter.

OIL PRESSURE WARNING LIGHT

The oil can symbol is another crucial warning sign. It indicates low oil pressure, which could be a sign of low oil levels or a more serious problem like an oil pump failure. Ignoring this symbol can lead to severe engine damage, so it's important to pull over and check your oil levels if it lights up.

ABS LIGHT

The ABS symbol, which usually looks like the letters "ABS" in a circle, refers to the anti-lock braking system. If this light comes on, it could mean there's a problem with the system that prevents your brakes from locking up during sudden stops, so you'll want to get that checked as soon as possible.

What Do the Different Colors on Flagpole Ropes Mean?

While most of us focus on the flags themselves, the ropes used to raise and lower the flags—called halyards—can also have different colors, and sometimes those colors carry special meaning. In some places, particularly in military or government settings, the color of the halyard can indicate rank or significance.

MILITARY AND GOVERNMENT FLAGPOLES

In military contexts, the halyard might be color-coded to reflect the rank of the person flying the flag. For example:

- •Gold or yellow ropes are sometimes used for high-ranking officials or ceremonial flagpoles.

- •Silver ropes could represent a lower rank or secondary importance.

These ropes can add an extra layer of symbolism, especially during formal events or ceremonies where every detail has meaning.

DECORATIVE OR FUNCTIONAL USE

In other cases, the colors of the halyards can simply be decorative or used to distinguish between different poles when there are multiple flags flying in the same area. For instance, some companies or organizations may choose halyard colors to match their branding, or to make it easier to identify which rope controls which flag.

MATERIALS AND DURABILITY

In addition to color, halyards can vary in materials, which affect their strength and weather resistance. You might see:

→

- White nylon or polyester ropes, which are common for their durability and resistance to weather.
- Colored ropes like red, blue, or green may be used for aesthetic reasons but also offer UV resistance to prevent fading.

Why Are There Bumps on the 'F' and 'J' Keys?

If you've ever noticed the small raised bumps on the 'F' and 'J' keys of your keyboard, you might wonder what they're there for. These tiny features are actually designed to help you find the home row without looking at the keyboard, making typing more efficient for those using the touch typing method.

THE HOME ROW

The home row is the middle row of letters on a **QWERTY** keyboard, where your fingers naturally rest. For touch typists—people who type without looking at the keyboard—the bumps on the 'F' and 'J' keys serve as reference points for the index fingers. Once your index fingers are placed on these bumps, your other fingers can easily find the right keys for the rest of the home row: 'A', 'S', 'D', 'K', 'L', and the semicolon.

WHY THEY'RE USEFUL

The bumps are designed so you can feel them, making it easier to locate the correct finger positions without glancing down. This helps you type faster and more accurately by maintaining your focus on the screen. It's a small but important feature that significantly improves typing speed and reduces errors.

WHERE YOU'LL FIND THEM

You'll find these bumps on most standard keyboards, whether for desktop computers, laptops, or even some tablet accessories. The design has become a universal feature for **QWERTY** keyboards, helping millions of typists navigate their keyboards every day.

How to Quickly Silence Your Phone in a Pinch

We've all been there: your phone goes off at the worst possible moment—during a meeting, in a quiet theater, or at the library. Silencing it quickly can feel stressful, but most smartphones have built-in shortcuts to make it easy.

On iPhones, there's a dedicated mute switch on the side of the phone. Flicking it to silent mode will instantly mute all sounds and notifications. This is especially useful because it allows you to silence your phone without even waking up the screen.

For Android users, many phones also have a volume-down shortcut.

Pressing and holding the volume down button for a few seconds or until you see the sound icon change to silent mode is a quick fix. Some Android models allow you to press the power and volume buttons simultaneously, which instantly activates silent mode.

Another handy tip for both platforms is setting your phone to automatically enter silent or "Do Not Disturb" mode during scheduled times. You can set these in your phone's settings, ensuring your phone stays quiet during meetings, appointments, or at bedtime.

By knowing these tricks, you can avoid the scramble to silence your phone in awkward situations, and you'll always stay in control of your phone's sounds.

Why Do Grocery Carts Have That One Wobbly Wheel?

The dreaded wobbly shopping cart wheel—it's a small annoyance that can make a simple trip to the grocery store frustrating. But why does it happen so often? It's all due to a mechanical issue called caster shimmy.

Shopping cart wheels are mounted on casters, which allow them to swivel freely in any direction. However, if the caster becomes loose, misaligned, or worn out, it causes the wheel to vibrate uncontrollably. This vibration happens because the wheel isn't making proper contact with the ground or isn't rotating smoothly. This can lead to that familiar wobbling sensation where the cart feels like it's fighting against you.

While there's no perfect fix as a shopper, applying even pressure on the cart can sometimes stabilize it. Many stores replace their cart wheels regularly to prevent this issue, but it's common for carts with heavy use to develop this problem quickly.

For grocery store owners, maintaining carts and ensuring the wheels are well-lubricated and properly aligned can reduce the number of wobbly carts, leading to a better shopping experience.

The Best Way to Clean Foggy Headlights

If your car's headlights have turned cloudy or yellow over time, they're not just unsightly—they can also reduce your visibility on the road, making driving at night more dangerous. Headlight lenses are typically made from polycarbonate plastic, which is durable but susceptible to oxidation from exposure to sunlight and environmental elements.

To restore your headlights to their former clarity, you don't necessarily need to buy an expensive restoration kit. One surprisingly effective home remedy is toothpaste. Toothpaste contains mild abrasives that can buff away the top layer of oxidation, much like sandpaper would but in a gentler form.

Here's how to clean your headlights with toothpaste:

1. Squeeze a generous amount of toothpaste onto a soft cloth or sponge.
2. Rub the toothpaste in circular motions over the foggy area of the headlight.
3. Continue scrubbing for a few minutes, making sure to cover the entire surface.
4. Rinse off the toothpaste with water and wipe the headlight clean.

For more lasting results, you can follow up with a UV-resistant sealant, which will protect the plastic from further sun damage.

Using toothpaste as a headlight cleaner is a quick, affordable fix that can make a noticeable difference in your car's appearance and your safety on the road.

How to Avoid ATM Fees

ATM fees can add up quickly if you're not careful. In fact, many banks charge non-customers fees that range from $2 to $5 per transaction, and your own bank may tack on additional charges for using out-of-network ATMs. But there are several ways you can avoid these annoying extra costs.

One of the easiest ways to avoid ATM fees is to plan ahead and use ATMs affiliated with your bank or credit union. Most major banks are part of nationwide ATM networks, allowing you to withdraw cash at no additional cost even if you're far from home. These ATMs are often found in grocery stores, gas stations, or pharmacies. A quick look at your bank's mobile app can help you locate the nearest fee-free ATM.

If you can't find an affiliated ATM nearby, a simple workaround is to request cash back when making a purchase at a store. Many retailers, especially grocery stores, allow you to withdraw extra cash during a debit card transaction, and they typically won't charge a fee for this service. This can save you a trip to the ATM and help you avoid those unnecessary charges.

For frequent travelers, consider opening a checking account that reimburses ATM fees. Some banks and online financial institutions offer accounts that automatically refund any fees you incur from out-of-network ATM transactions, making them a great option for people on the go.

By being proactive and planning your cash withdrawals, you can save a surprising amount of money on ATM fees over time.

Why Do Clocks Run Clockwise?

Imagine the world before mechanical clocks existed—where people relied on nature to track time. The first timekeepers were sundials, instruments that tracked the sun's shadow as it moved across the sky. In the Northern Hemisphere, the shadow on a sundial naturally moves from left to right, and that's what early humans used to measure the passing of hours. But here's where it gets fascinating: if clocks had been invented in the Southern Hemisphere, our clocks might run in the opposite direction!

When mechanical clocks came into fashion in 14th century Europe, clockmakers mimicked this left-to-right motion in the design of the clock hands. They made the hands rotate in what we now call "clockwise," simply because it felt natural to follow the path of the sun's shadow. It became the global standard, passed down from medieval monks to modern-day engineers. This subtle connection between nature and human design is ingrained in every ticking clock you see today.

But think about this: it's all a product of where humans first observed the sun's patterns. If those early clockmakers had lived in the Southern Hemisphere, where shadows move the opposite way, we'd live in a world where time literally runs backward—or rather, counterclockwise! So every time you check your watch, you're witnessing a small piece of ancient human history in action.

Why Are There Dimples on a Golf Ball?

If you've ever looked closely at a golf ball, you'll notice its surface is covered with dimples. These dimples aren't just for design—they play a vital role in how the ball travels through the air. In fact, without dimples, a golf ball wouldn't travel nearly as far or accurately. Here's why.

THE ROLE OF DIMPLES IN AERODYNAMICS

When a smooth ball moves through the air, it creates a layer of turbulent airflow around its surface. This air sticks to the ball longer, increasing drag (air resistance) and slowing the ball down. However, dimples on a golf ball change how the air flows around it. By creating turbulence, the dimples force the air to cling closer to the surface of the ball for a longer time, reducing drag. Less drag allows the ball to travel farther, even when struck with the same force.

DIMPLES AND LIFT

Dimples also affect the lift of a golf ball. When the ball spins, it spin to make the ball curve, stop quickly on the green, or roll farther.

THE SCIENCE BEHIND THE NUMBERS

Most modern golf balls have between 300 and 500 dimples, which is the optimal range to balance distance and control. The depth and shape of the dimples can also vary, with some dimple pattern can make a noticeable difference in the ball's flight.

In short, the dimples on a golf ball aren't just for looks—they're an essential part of the ball's aerodynamics, helping it fly farther, higher, and with more control than a smooth ball ever could.

Why Do We Crave Junk Food When We're Tired?

It's a familiar scenario: you didn't get enough sleep, and suddenly, you're reaching for cookies, chips, or anything sugary and salty. This craving isn't just about comfort; it's rooted in how sleep deprivation affects your body's hormones and energy needs.

HORMONAL IMBALANCE: GHRELIN AND LEPTIN

When you're tired, the hormones that regulate hunger—ghrelin and leptin—get out of balance. Ghrelin is known as the hunger hormone; it tells your brain when you're hungry. When you're sleep-deprived, your ghrelin levels increase, making you feel hungrier than usual. On the other hand, leptin is the hormone responsible for making you feel full, and its levels drop when you haven't had enough rest. This combination of higher ghrelin and lower leptin results in powerful hunger cues, especially for high-calorie foods.

QUICK ENERGY FIX: SUGARY AND FATTY FOODS

When you're low on energy, your brain seeks out quick fixes to give you an immediate boost. Sugary and fatty foods provide a rapid spike in blood sugar, giving your brain the quick energy it's craving. Unfortunately, this is often a temporary fix, and once the blood sugar spike wears off, you might feel even more tired and find yourself craving more junk food.

THE REWARD SYSTEM

Sleep deprivation also affects your brain's reward system. When you're tired, the brain's prefrontal cortex, which is responsible for making rational decisions, isn't functioning as efficiently. Meanwhile, your brain's reward center becomes more active, making you more likely to reach for pleasure-inducing junk foods that activate the release of dopamine, the "feel-good" chemical. The brain knows that foods high in sugar, fat, or salt will give it a dopamine boost, which is why those cravings are harder to resist when you're sleep-deprived.

LACK OF SLEEP DISRUPTS METABOLISM

Sleep deprivation not only messes with your hunger hormones but also affects how your

body processes calories. Studies show that when you're tired, your metabolism slows down, and your body becomes less efficient at processing and burning calories. This means your body is more likely to store those extra calories from junk food as fat, compounding the effects of sleep deprivation.

In short, a lack of sleep creates the perfect storm of hormonal changes, energy crashes, and reward-seeking behavior that drives you toward junk food. So, the next time you're feeling sleep-deprived and craving something unhealthy, just know it's your body trying to cope with the imbalance.

Why Do Alarm Clocks Always Seem to Go Off Right When You're in Deep Sleep?

It can feel almost cruel when your alarm goes off, and you're jolted awake, still feeling groggy and disoriented. This grogginess often happens because the alarm interrupted you during a period of deep sleep, the stage of sleep that leaves you feeling the most rested—and yet, the hardest to wake from.

THE SCIENCE OF SLEEP CYCLES

Your body goes through several sleep cycles each night, with each cycle lasting about 90 minutes. These cycles alternate between light sleep, REM sleep (rapid eye movement), and deep sleep (also known as slow-wave sleep). Deep sleep is the most restorative stage, where your body repairs muscles, boosts the immune system, and consolidates memories.

When your alarm wakes you during deep sleep, your brain hasn't finished its restorative work, and you may feel disoriented or groggy as a result. This feeling is called sleep inertia, and it can last for a few minutes to a couple of hours, making it harder to get going in the morning.

WHY DOES IT ALWAYS SEEM TO HAPPEN DURING DEEP SLEEP?

Because sleep cycles are predictable, your alarm could, by chance, go off during deep sleep, depending on when you went to bed and how many cycles you've completed. Most people have 4 to 6 cycles minimizing that groggy feeling.

per night. If your sleep schedule is irregular, you're more likely to be caught in the middle of deep sleep when the alarm sounds.

SLEEP TRACKERS AND SMART ALARMS

Modern sleep trackers and smart alarms aim to address this issue by waking you during a lighter stage of sleep. They monitor your movement and heart rate to estimate where you are in your sleep cycle and wake you up when you're closer to the surface of wakefulness.

So, the next time your alarm feels like it's set to disrupt your deepest rest, it's really just bad timing—sleep cycles are natural, and unfortunately, alarms don't know the difference between REM and deep sleep unless they're specifically designed to track it.

Why Do Dogs Tilt Their Heads When You Talk to Them?

Dogs have an adorable habit of tilting their heads to the side when you speak to them, and while it might look like they're simply being cute, there's actually more to it than that. This behavior is thought to be a combination of curiosity, communication, and anatomy.

IMPROVED HEARING

One theory is that dogs tilt their heads to improve their ability to hear and locate sounds. Dogs have a remarkable sense of hearing, but the way their ears are positioned can affect how they perceive sound direction. By tilting their heads, dogs may be adjusting their ears to better pinpoint where a sound is coming from or to hear certain tones more clearly. This is especially true when dogs hear high-pitched or unfamiliar sounds, such as the way humans talk to them.

READING BODY LANGUAGE

Dogs are also highly attuned to visual cues. When a dog tilts its head, it might be trying to get a better view of your facial expressions or body language, which helps them understand what you're communicating. Some dogs may have longer muzzles that partially block their view, so tilting their heads gives them a clearer perspective on your face, allowing them to read your emotions and intentions more accurately.

SOCIAL INTERACTION

Dogs are experts at picking up on social cues from humans, and they know that certain behaviors, like tilting their heads, elicit a positive response from their owners. If you frequently respond with praise or affection when your dog tilts its head, they may do it more often as a way to communicate or get your attention. This behavior can be a learned response, driven by the desire to interact with you.

It's just one more way dogs show us how attentive they are to everything we say and do!

UNDERSTANDING SPEECH

Another reason dogs tilt their heads could be related to their attempts to understand speech. Dogs are capable of recognizing certain words and phrases, and they may tilt their heads to focus on the sound of your voice or try to pick up on familiar cues. This is their way of concentrating on what you're saying, as they try to decipher what words or commands they know.

Ultimately, this endearing behavior is likely a combination of practical adjustments for better hearing, an effort to read facial cues, and a way of engaging with their human companions.

Why Are Phone Chargers So Short?

If you've ever found yourself wishing your phone charger cable was longer, you're not alone. Many phone chargers come with relatively short cables, and there are a few reasons behind this design choice, ranging from practicality to performance.

FASTER CHARGING WITH SHORTER CABLES

One of the key reasons phone chargers are so short is that shorter cables are more efficient at delivering power. With a shorter cable, there's less resistance for the electrical current to travel through, which means your phone charges faster. The longer a cable is, the more resistance it introduces, which can slow down the charging speed. Shorter cables minimize this issue, allowing the charger to deliver power to your phone more effectively and quickly.

REDUCING VOLTAGE DROP

When current travels through a longer cable, some of the voltage is lost due to resistance in the wire, a phenomenon known as voltage drop. This can lead to slower charging and a less efficient transfer of power. By keeping the cable short, manufacturers help prevent this voltage drop, ensuring that your phone gets the most power possible, especially when fast charging is involved.

PORTABILITY AND CONVENIENCE

Phone chargers are designed to be portable and convenient. A short cable is easier to carry around, pack in a bag, or store in your car without getting tangled. While it might be less convenient for use across a large room, a short cable is much more practical for charging your phone on the go, especially when you're traveling or commuting.

WIRELESS CHARGING AND LONG-TERM TRENDS

As wireless charging technology becomes more common, the length of charging cables may matter less in the future. But for now, short cables are a compromise between efficiency, cost, and portability.

Manufacturing Costs

There's also the factor of cost. Shorter cables require less material to manufacture, making them cheaper to produce. For manufacturers that produce millions of units, the savings from using less copper, plastic, and other materials can be significant. Shorter cables are also easier to package and ship, reducing overall costs for the company.

Why Do Some Glasses Make Drinks Taste Better?

The shape of a glass might seem like a small detail, but it can have a surprisingly big impact on how a drink tastes and how you experience it. The reason lies in a combination of science and design. Different types of drinks interact with air, temperature, and the glass surface in ways that can enhance or mute their flavors. Here's why the glass you choose matters:

SURFACE AREA AND AROMA

One of the biggest reasons certain drinks taste better in specific

glasses is because of how the glass affects the aroma. Wine glasses are a perfect example of this. The larger bowl of a wine glass allows more air to come into contact with the surface of the wine, which releases the aromas. When you swirl wine in the glass, more oxygen is mixed in, and this helps to "open up" the wine's flavors. Since your sense of smell plays a huge role in how you perceive taste, a properly shaped wine glass makes it easier to appreciate the subtleties in the drink's flavor profile.

DIRECTING THE FLOW OF THE LIQUID

Another important factor is how the glass directs the flow of liquid to your mouth. For example, the rim of a whiskey glass is often designed to be wider, which allows the liquid to hit your tongue at different angles, giving you a more rounded taste of the drink's complexities. A narrower rim might funnel the liquid directly to a specific part of your mouth, emphasizing different notes.

Certain glasses are even designed to control how much of the drink comes into contact with your taste buds at once, which can change your perception of the drink's body and flavor. In this way, the shape of the glass can make a drink feel more balanced or highlight different flavor layers.

TEMPERATURE AND INSULATION

The material and thickness of a glass can also affect how a drink tastes by influencing its temperature. Thicker glasses, or those with double-walled designs, help keep hot drinks like coffee or tea at their ideal temperature for longer, which prevents them from becoming bitter as they cool. Similarly, a thin-rimmed glass can make cold drinks, like a crisp white wine, feel lighter and more refreshing as the thin glass doesn't hold much heat.

VISUAL APPEAL

While the look of a glass doesn't change the drink's chemistry, there's no denying that the visual appeal of a drink served in a well-designed glass enhances the overall experience. Part of the pleasure of drinking, especially with cocktails, wine, or champagne, is the presentation. A beautifully shaped glass makes the drink feel more special and can set the tone for how you enjoy it. This psychological aspect is an often overlooked but important part of why some glasses make drinks taste better.

Why Do Cats Knock Things Over?

If you've ever owned a cat, you've probably witnessed them swat something off a table or counter, only to watch with apparent satisfaction as it crashes to the floor. But why do they do this? It turns out, cats aren't just being mischievous—they're often acting on natural instincts and curiosity.

HUNTING BEHAVIOR

At their core, cats are predators, and their instincts are deeply tied to hunting and exploring. In the wild, a cat might bat at its prey to see if it moves or makes a sound. This same behavior translates to your home, where objects like pens, cups, or even phones can become "prey." By swatting at an object, your cat is mimicking the action of testing potential prey to see if it responds or can be caught.

CURIOSITY AND EXPLORATION

Cats are naturally curious creatures, and knocking things over is a way for them to explore their environment. Since they don't have hands like humans, their primary way of interacting with objects is through their paws. When they encounter something new, they'll often bat at it to see what happens. Will it fall? Make a noise? Is it something they can play with or hunt?

This curiosity-driven behavior helps them understand the world around them, even if it sometimes results in broken items or spilled liquids. To a cat, knocking over objects is a form of investigation—an attempt to learn more about how objects behave.

ATTENTION-SEEKING

Another possible explanation is that your cat has learned that
knocking things over gets a reaction. Cats are incredibly observant,
and they quickly learn what behaviors will get them attention, whether
positive or negative. If every time your cat knocks something over, you
rush over to scold them or clean up the mess, they might start doing it
simply because they've learned it will get your attention.

BOREDOM OR PLAYFULNESS

Sometimes, knocking things over is just a way for cats to entertain
themselves. If a cat is feeling bored or playful, batting objects off a
surface can be a fun game. It's a form of self-entertainment, especially
if they don't have enough toys or stimulation to keep them occupied.

Why Do Some Pots and Pans Have Holes in the Handles?

At first glance, the hole at the end of a pot or pan handle might seem like a simple design for hanging cookware. While that's certainly one of its purposes, the hole actually serves another clever function that not everyone is aware of: it's designed to hold a cooking utensil.

A SPOON REST IN DISGUISE

When you're cooking, it's common to reach for a spoon or spatula to stir or serve your food. Instead of placing the utensil on the counter, where it can leave a mess, the hole in the handle provides a convenient place to rest your spoon. By sliding the handle of the spoon or spatula into the hole, you can rest the utensil directly over the pot or pan, allowing any sauce or liquid to drip back into the food instead of onto your countertop.

VERSATILITY FOR STORAGE AND COOKING

While the hole's primary purpose is often thought to be for hanging the pan on a rack or hook for storage, this dual-purpose design is a small but smart feature that enhances both organization and cleanliness while cooking. It's a detail that makes kitchen tasks just a bit more convenient, especially when you're multitasking or dealing with limited counter space.

Why Do Elevator "Close Door" Buttons Often Not Work?

You've probably pressed the "close door" button in an elevator at some point, only to feel like it didn't make a difference. As it turns out, in many cases, you're right. The "close door" button is often more about providing a sense of control than actually speeding up the door's closing.

MODERN ELEVATORS: THE BUTTON AS A PLACEBO

In most modern elevators, especially in buildings constructed after the 1990s, the "close door" button is either deactivated or programmed to function only for emergency personnel. These buttons are part of what's known as placebo buttons—features in devices that offer the illusion of control but don't significantly alter the machine's function for most users. The idea is that people are more satisfied and less anxious when they believe they can influence their environment.

The "close door" button, in many cases, is required to work only for firefighters or maintenance workers who need to use it in emergency situations. These professionals often have access to a special key or override switch that activates the button. For everyone else, the doors will close on their own after a short delay, regardless of whether the button is pressed.

WHY DISABLE THE BUTTON?

The decision to deactivate or limit the function of the button largely comes down to safety and accessibility. Elevator doors are designed to stay open long enough to allow everyone, including those with mobility issues, time to safely enter and exit. Reducing the door delay could pose a risk to passengers who need a bit more time. By preventing the button from closing the door early, elevator manufacturers help ensure that no one is accidentally left behind or injured by a door closing too quickly.

A HOLDOVER FROM EARLIER DESIGNS

Older elevator systems often had fully functional "close door" buttons that worked for all passengers. In these elevators, pressing the button would immediately start the closing process, but as safety regulations became stricter, the function was removed or restricted in newer models. Despite this, the button remains in elevators more as a familiar fixture than a functional control, contributing to the user's sense of interaction with the elevator.

So, while you might think you're speeding up the process when you press that button, chances are it's just a bit of wishful thinking.

Why Are Some Electrical Outlets Upside Down?

If you've ever noticed that some electrical outlets seem to be installed "upside down," with the ground prong at the top instead of the bottom, it's not a mistake or random choice. This small but purposeful change has to do with safety.

THE GROUND-UP INSTALLATION FOR SAFETY

When an outlet is installed with the ground prong (the round hole at the bottom of a typical outlet) at the top, it's meant to prevent electrical accidents. Here's why:

Imagine something metal, like a loose plug, falling toward the outlet while it's in use. If the ground prong is at the top, the metal object is more likely to hit the ground first, which reduces the risk of a short circuit or sparking. If the metal hits the hot or neutral prongs first (which are the two vertical slots), it could cause an electrical hazard, like a shock or fire.

WHEN YOU MIGHT SEE THIS

You're more likely to find upside-down outlets in places where safety is a concern, such as kitchens, workshops, or commercial buildings, where electrical code might recommend ground-up installation. In some regions, it's even required by local building codes for specific installations.

THE "RIGHT WAY" TO INSTALL OUTLETS?

There's actually no national electrical code requirement in the U.S. for whether outlets should be installed ground-up or ground-down. It's mostly up to the preference of the electrician or the homeowner.

However, many electricians choose the ground-up method for peace of mind in areas where a plugged-in device might come in contact with other objects.

Why Do Some Metal Objects Feel Colder Than Others at the Same Temperature?

You've likely noticed that metal objects feel much colder than wooden or plastic ones, even when they're all sitting in the same room. The reason behind this sensation lies in the science of thermal conductivity. Metal is an excellent conductor of heat, meaning it transfers heat very efficiently compared to other materials. When you touch a metal object, heat from your skin is quickly drawn into the metal, making it feel cold, even though it's the same temperature as everything else around it.

In contrast, materials like wood and plastic are insulators. They don't transfer heat as well, so when you touch them, your body doesn't lose heat as quickly, and they feel warmer by comparison. This principle explains why a metal chair in winter feels much colder than a wooden one, even though both are exposed to the same conditions.

This difference in thermal conductivity isn't just about comfort—it's the same reason metals are used for things like radiators and cooking pans. Their ability to transfer heat quickly makes them invaluable in situations where efficient heat exchange is needed. So the next time you shiver at the touch of cold metal, remember, it's just physics at work!

Why Does Salt Make Ice Colder?

You've probably noticed that salt gets sprinkled on icy roads to melt ice in the winter, but did you know that salt can also make ice colder? This is why salt is commonly used in ice cream makers and cooling mixtures—it helps lower the temperature of ice, making it more effective at freezing things quickly.

THE SCIENCE BEHIND IT: FREEZING POINT DEPRESSION

Salt lowers the freezing point of water, a phenomenon called freezing point depression. Normally, water freezes at 32°F (0°C), but when you add salt, it disrupts the bonds between water molecules, making it harder for the ice to maintain its solid state. As a result, the temperature at which the water freezes drops.

When you sprinkle salt on ice, the ice begins to melt, but because the temperature is still below freezing, the water can't remain a liquid for long. As the ice melts, heat is absorbed from the surroundings, creating a cooling effect. This process continues until the ice reaches a much lower temperature than it would if left alone.

WHY DOES THIS MAKE ICE COLDER?

While the ice melts, the mixture of ice and salt water becomes significantly colder than regular ice. This is because the salt forces the ice to absorb more heat from the environment (or from whatever it's in contact with) to keep melting. For example, when you're making homemade ice cream, the salt-ice mixture around the ice cream container can drop to as low as -6°F (-21°C). This super-chilled mixture helps freeze the ice cream faster and more evenly.

PRACTICAL USES

• Melting ice on roads: When salt is spread on icy roads, it lowers the freezing point of the ice, causing it to melt even in cold temperatures, which helps prevent accidents.

• Ice cream makers: Salt is used with ice to lower the temperature around the ice cream mixture, ensuring it freezes more quickly.

• Cooling beverages: If you want to chill drinks faster, placing them in a cooler with ice and adding salt can speed up the cooling process.

In essence, adding salt to ice forces the ice to get even colder by lowering the freezing point and pulling heat from its surroundings, which is why it's such an effective method for rapid cooling.

Why Do We Say "Bless You" When Someone Sneezes?

Saying "Bless you" when someone sneezes is one of those reflexive phrases we use without giving it much thought. But where does this tradition come from, and why do we say it in response to sneezing, of all things?

THE PLAGUE AND SUPERSTITIONS

One of the most widely believed origins of saying "Bless you" dates back to the 6th century, during the reign of Pope Gregory I. During that time, the bubonic plague was sweeping through Europe, and sneezing was thought to be one of the early symptoms. To prevent the spread of illness, the Pope encouraged people to say "God bless you" after someone sneezed, hoping that the invocation of divine protection might help prevent the onset of the disease. This practice quickly spread and became ingrained in European culture.

Another superstition around sneezing involved the belief that sneezing expelled a person's soul from their body, leaving them momentarily vulnerable to evil spirits. Saying "Bless you" was thought to protect the person from harm and help keep their soul intact. Conversely, some believed that sneezing could cause the devil to enter the body, and a blessing was a way to ward off this threat.

THE HEART-STOP MYTH

Another commonly cited myth is the idea that your heart stops when you sneeze, and saying

"Bless you" was a way of celebrating the fact that you survived the sneeze and your heart started beating again. While this is a charming thought, it's scientifically inaccurate—your heart does not stop when you sneeze. However, the intensity of a sneeze can momentarily change your heart rhythm due to the pressure in your chest, which might have contributed to the idea.

CULTURAL VARIATIONS

Interestingly, different cultures have their own versions of this phrase. In Germany, people say "Gesundheit," which means "health." Similarly, in some cultures, phrases used after sneezing directly relate to wishing the person good health or recovery, reinforcing the idea that sneezing might signal the beginning of illness.

Whether it's out of concern for health, an old superstition, or just politeness, saying "Bless you" has stuck around for centuries, making it one of those small but interesting traditions that connect us to the past.

What's the Difference Between Baking Powder and Baking Soda?

Both baking powder and baking soda are essential ingredients in baking, but they're not interchangeable. Understanding the difference between these two common leavening agents can make or break a recipe.

BAKING SODA

Baking soda, or sodium bicarbonate, is a base that needs an acid to activate it. When baking soda is mixed with something acidic—like lemon juice, vinegar, buttermilk, or yogurt—it creates a chemical reaction that produces carbon dioxide gas. This gas forms tiny bubbles in the dough or batter, which helps it rise and become light and fluffy.

Since baking soda is pure alkaline, it will only work if your recipe includes an acidic ingredient. Without that acid, the baking soda won't create the necessary gas, and your baked goods could end up flat or with an odd, soapy taste. Baking soda also acts quickly, so it's important to get your mixture into the oven right away after combining it with an acid to maximize the leavening effect.

BAKING POWDER

Baking powder contains both sodium bicarbonate (the same base as baking soda) and an acid, usually in the form of cream of tartar. Because the acid is already mixed in, baking powder doesn't need an additional acidic ingredient to activate. All it needs is moisture and heat to start the leavening process. This makes baking powder more versatile and easier to use in recipes that don't have acidic ingredients.

There are two types of baking powder:

- Single-acting: This type activates as soon as it gets wet, meaning you need to bake immediately after mixing.

- Double-acting: The more common type, double-acting baking powder releases gas in two stages—once when it's mixed with liquid, and again when it's exposed to heat in the oven. This gives a more consistent rise and allows you a bit more flexibility in timing. When to Use Each

Many recipes call for both baking soda and baking powder. This is because baking soda provides the quick lift needed at the start of the baking process, while baking powder gives a longer, more sustained rise. Additionally, baking soda helps neutralize acidic ingredients, balancing the flavor, while baking powder ensures you get the right texture and height.

If a recipe calls for baking powder and you only have baking soda, you can substitute, but you'll need to add an acidic ingredient to get the desired effect. If you're substituting baking soda for baking powder, you'll also need to adjust the amounts, as baking soda is much stronger than baking powder.

What Do the Numbers on a Toaster Dial Really Mean?

Most people assume the numbers on a toaster dial represent the level of toastiness or how dark their bread will get. But in reality, those numbers are typically tied to time, not the temperature or darkness level of the toast. When you set your toaster to a certain number, say "3," you're usually setting the toaster to toast the bread for approximately three minutes, not to reach a certain degree of crispiness.

TIME, NOT TEMPERATURE

Each toaster model can vary slightly, but in general, the numbers indicate how long the toaster will apply heat to the bread. A setting

of "1" will toast for a short time, while a higher number, like "5," will keep the heating elements on for a longer period. The darkness of your toast is really a result of how long the bread is exposed to that heat. So, if you like your toast light and golden, you'd pick a lower number, which will result in a shorter toasting time.

THE VARIABLES

There are also a number of factors that can affect how your toast turns out, even if you're using the same time setting each day. For example, the type of bread you're toasting matters—a thicker slice or one with more moisture (like sourdough) will need more time to toast than a thin, dry slice (like white sandwich bread). Additionally, if you're toasting multiple batches of bread, your toaster is already preheated from the first batch, so subsequent slices will toast faster.

Knowing that toaster dials are essentially timers gives you better control over how you toast different types of bread. If you need a quick toast or are reheating a previously toasted slice, using a lower setting can help prevent your toast from burning. On the other hand, for more moisture-rich breads, you might want to increase the dial setting to ensure the bread gets evenly toasted.

Why Do Woodworkers Use Wood Glue and Nails Together?

In woodworking, combining wood glue and nails (or screws) is a time-tested method for creating strong, long-lasting joints. While either glue or nails could technically hold pieces of wood together, using them in tandem offers several significant advantages in terms of strength, durability, and alignment.

THE STRENGTH OF WOOD GLUE

Wood glue is one of the strongest adhesives available for woodworking, and when used properly, it can create joints that are often stronger than the wood itself. When you apply wood glue, it penetrates the wood fibers, creating a bond that chemically hardens as it cures. Once fully set, the glue forms a rigid connection that can resist both tension (pulling forces) and compression (pressing forces).

However, glue requires time to cure, and during this curing period, the wood pieces are vulnerable to shifting, especially if they are under any stress. This is particularly true with larger or heavier components, where even a small amount of movement can compromise the alignment of the pieces and weaken the bond.

THE ROLE OF NAILS OR SCREWS

This is where nails or screws come into play. Their primary role is to provide immediate mechanical strength, holding the pieces in place while the glue dries. Think of nails as temporary clamps that hold the project together while the glue works its magic.

Nails or screws ensure that the pieces remain perfectly aligned during assembly and prevent any shifting or movement that could occur before the glue sets. This combination is especially important when working on complex projects where clamps may not be able to reach every corner or where the joint needs immediate reinforcement.

SHEAR VS. TENSILE STRENGTH

One of the key benefits of using both wood glue and nails is that they complement each other in terms of the types of forces they can withstand. Glue provides excellent tensile strength, meaning it resists forces that would pull the pieces of wood apart. Nails, on the other hand, offer high shear strength, which means they resist forces trying to slide the two pieces of wood in different directions.

When combined, the glue creates a strong, rigid bond that handles pulling forces, while the nails reinforce the joint against sliding forces. Together, they create a joint that is more robust than either fastener alone, providing superior durability.

Long-Term Durability

As the glue cures and solidifies, it forms the permanent bond that will provide the majority of the joint's strength over time. Once the glue is fully cured, the nails or screws act as reinforcement, ensuring that the bond remains intact, even if the project is subject to stress, vibration, or environmental changes like expansion and contraction due to humidity.

This method is widely used in projects that require long-term durability, such as furniture, cabinetry, or structural elements. While glue is the primary agent for holding the joint together, the nails ensure that the bond is as secure as possible right from the start, which is crucial for heavier projects or parts that will bear weight.

When to Use Just Glue or Nails

In some cases, woodworkers may opt to use only glue, especially in fine woodworking where visible nails or screws would detract from the appearance of the finished piece. Clamps are often used in these cases to hold the pieces together while the glue dries, but this method can be more time-consuming and less practical for large-scale projects.

Conversely, in rough carpentry or construction, nails or screws may be used without glue when quick assembly is needed, and aesthetics are less of a concern. However, for most woodworking projects where both strength and appearance matter, the combination of glue and nails provides the best of both worlds.

What Are Wood Grains, and Why Do They Matter?

Wood grain refers to the pattern and direction of fibers in a piece of wood, and understanding it is crucial for woodworkers. Grain patterns form as the tree grows, with fibers aligning along the direction of growth. The grain impacts the wood's strength, workability, and appearance.

DIFFERENT TYPES OF GRAIN

- → •Straight Grain: This is the most common and easiest to work with. The fibers run parallel to the length of the board, making it easier to cut, plane, and sand. Straight grain is also more stable and less likely to warp or twist over time.

- → •Curly Grain: Some trees, like maple, develop a wavy or curly grain, which creates beautiful visual effects. However, it's harder to work with because the irregular grain can cause the wood to tear out during planing or cutting.

- → •Knotty Grain: Found in woods like pine, knots can create unique designs in the wood. However, knots are generally weaker than the surrounding wood and can cause structural weaknesses, especially if they appear in load-bearing areas.

WHY WOOD GRAIN MATTERS

The direction of the grain determines how wood reacts when you work with it. For example, cutting against the grain can cause tear-out, where fibers splinter or break away unevenly, leaving rough, unsightly edges. Cutting or planing with the grain, however, allows for a smoother, cleaner cut.

Wood grain also influences how well the wood absorbs stain and finish. Open-grain woods like oak or ash have more prominent pores, which allow stain to penetrate deeply and create rich color. Closed-grain woods like maple or cherry have a smoother surface, which results in a more even, lighter finish.

By understanding wood grain, woodworkers can choose the right wood for the job, make accurate cuts, and achieve the best possible finish, both aesthetically and structurally.

What's the Difference Between Hardwoods and Softwoods?

At first glance, you might assume that hardwoods are always harder and denser than softwoods, but the difference between these two types of wood is actually based on the type of tree they come from, not necessarily the wood's density or hardness.

HARDWOODS

Hardwoods come from deciduous trees, which are trees that lose their leaves annually, such as oak, maple, cherry, and walnut. These trees tend to grow more slowly, which results in a denser grain structure, making them generally harder and more durable. However, the term hardwood doesn't always mean the wood is harder—there are some hardwoods, like basswood or poplar, that are softer than some softwoods. Hardwoods are commonly used for furniture, flooring, and high-end cabinetry, as their durability and attractive grain make them ideal for projects that require strength and aesthetic appeal.

SOFTWOODS

Softwoods, on the other hand, come from coniferous trees, which are evergreens like pine, cedar, and spruce. These trees grow faster and produce a lighter, less dense grain compared to hardwoods. While many softwoods, like pine, are more prone to dents and scratches due to their softness, some softwoods, like Douglas fir, are actually quite strong and durable. Softwoods are often used in construction, framing, decking, and general carpentry because they are easy to work with, more readily available, and generally more affordable than hardwoods.

GRAIN STRUCTURE

The grain structure is one of the most noticeable differences between hardwoods and softwoods. Hardwoods typically have a tight grain pattern with small, dense pores, which

gives them a more refined and smooth finish when sanded and stained. Softwoods usually have a more open grain with larger growth rings, giving them a coarser appearance. These differences in grain also affect how each type of wood absorbs stains and finishes, with hardwoods generally offering more even coloring and richer finishes.

COMMON USES

- → •Hardwoods: Used for projects that require strength, longevity, and aesthetic quality, such as fine furniture, flooring, and high-quality cabinets.

- → •Softwoods: Commonly used for construction purposes, like framing houses, making plywood, or producing outdoor furniture.

Despite the names, it's important to remember that some softwoods can be harder than certain hardwoods, and each type has its own strengths depending on the project. Understanding the distinctions between the two helps woodworkers choose the right material for the job.

Why Are Manhole Covers Round?

When you think about manhole covers, you might notice that almost all of them are round. It's a design feature that might seem arbitrary at first, but there are several very practical reasons why manhole covers are circular instead of square or another shape.

THEY CAN'T FALL THROUGH THE HOLE

One of the main reasons manhole covers are round is because it's

the only shape that can't fall through the hole it's designed to cover. If a manhole cover were square or rectangular, it could be turned at an angle and potentially drop through the opening, which would be dangerous for workers below. A circular cover, however, has the same diameter all around, meaning it can never fall through the opening, regardless of how it's positioned.

or reposition compared to a square or rectangular cover, which would have to be lifted and carried. The round shape allows for

EASIER TO MOVE

Manhole covers are heavy, often weighing between 50 to 150 pounds. A circular cover can be rolled on its edge, making it easier to move more efficient handling when moving the cover off the manhole and back into place.

UNIFORM DISTRIBUTION OF PRESSURE

Round manhole covers are also stronger because the circular shape evenly distributes pressure from above. This is especially important for covers that need to withstand heavy vehicles passing over them. The round design helps prevent the cover from cracking or breaking under pressure, making it more durable than other shapes, which could have weaker corners.

SIMPLICITY IN MANUFACTURING

From a manufacturing standpoint, a round manhole cover is simpler to produce because there's no need to worry about alignment when placing it back over the hole. No matter how the cover is turned, it will always fit properly. This makes round covers more convenient and cost-effective to produce and install.

Ultimately, the round shape of manhole covers is a smart and practical solution that enhances safety, durability, and efficiency in both use and production. It's a perfect example of form following function in everyday design.

Why Are Carpenter Pencils Flat?

If you've ever used or seen a carpenter's pencil, you'll notice right away that it's unlike a regular pencil—it's flat and rectangular instead of round. This unique design isn't just for style; it's a brilliant example of form meeting function in the world of woodworking.

The flat shape of a carpenter's pencil serves two primary purposes:

1. IT PREVENTS ROLLING

One of the most practical reasons for the flat design is that it keeps the pencil from rolling away. On a busy job site or workbench, which is often uneven or sloped, a round pencil would easily roll off the surface, potentially getting lost or damaged. The flat shape ensures

the pencil stays where you leave it, which saves both time and frustration—especially in high-pressure work environments where every second counts.

2. IT'S EASIER TO GRIP AND MORE DURABLE

The thicker, flat body of the pencil is easier to grip and manipulate, even while wearing work gloves. Unlike traditional pencils, which can snap easily under pressure, the carpenter's pencil has a much thicker core of graphite, making it more resistant to breakage when you're marking rough surfaces like wood, drywall, or concrete.

Carpenters also appreciate the wide, flat lead for its ability to make both thick and thin lines, depending on how the pencil is angled. This flexibility is useful for a range of tasks, from drawing detailed measurements to making more visible, broader marks on construction materials. The thicker lead also lasts longer, meaning fewer

What's the Purpose of Pilot Holes in Woodworking?

In woodworking, drilling pilot holes before driving screws isn't just a suggestion—it's a critical step that ensures both the strength and appearance of your project. A pilot hole is a small hole drilled into a piece of wood to guide a screw or nail. But why is this seemingly simple step so important?

When you drive a screw directly into wood without a pilot hole, you're forcing the threads of the screw to carve their own path through the wood. This can put a lot of pressure on the wood fibers, especially in harder woods like oak or maple. In response to this pressure, the wood may split, particularly near the edges or in thinner pieces, creating unsightly cracks that weaken the structure of your project.

By drilling a pilot hole, you're giving the screw a predetermined path, reducing the stress on the wood. The hole provides enough space for the screw to enter smoothly without forcing the wood fibers apart. This keeps the wood intact and preserves the strength of your joint. The size of the pilot hole depends on the type and size of the screw— ideally, the pilot hole should be slightly smaller than the diameter of the screw's shaft, allowing the threads to grip the wood while minimizing stress.

PREVENTING STRIPPED SCREWS AND EASIER FASTENING

Another benefit of pilot holes is that they prevent stripped screws. When you try to force a screw into dense wood without a guide, you often have to apply a lot of pressure, which can wear down the screw's head, making it difficult to drive in further or remove if needed. Pilot holes make it easier to seat screws, allowing you to use less force and reduce the risk of damaging the screw head.

Pilot holes are also incredibly helpful when working with power tools, like a cordless drill or impact driver, by providing precision and reducing the effort required to fasten pieces together. For delicate projects or working with fragile hardwoods, drilling pilot holes ensures your screws go in cleanly and neatly, preserving the overall appearance of your work.

Why Do Microwave Ovens Have a Mesh Grid on the Door?

That mesh grid on your microwave door isn't just there for

aesthetics—it's a critical component of the microwave's safety features. The microwave oven works by emitting microwave radiation, a type of electromagnetic wave, that causes water molecules in food to vibrate rapidly, producing heat. But microwaves, being a form of radiation, could be dangerous if they leaked out into your kitchen.

The metal mesh on the microwave door prevents that from happening. The holes in the mesh are small enough that they block the microwaves from escaping, but they're large enough to let visible light through so you can still see your food cooking. This is because microwaves have a much longer wavelength than visible light (about 12 centimeters), so while the light passes through the holes, the microwaves are reflected back into the oven, where they can safely heat your food.

This simple yet effective design means you can stand right next to your microwave without worrying about exposure to harmful radiation, all while watching your leftovers heat up.

Why Is There a Hole in Pen Caps?

It might seem like a trivial feature, but that little hole in the top of many pen caps is actually designed to save lives. You may not give it much thought as you absentmindedly chew on your pen during a meeting, but should you accidentally swallow the cap, the hole serves a crucial purpose: it helps prevent choking.

The hole allows a small amount of air to pass through, even if the pen cap gets lodged in your throat. While the cap might still need to be removed by a doctor, the hole buys time, allowing you to breathe until medical help arrives. This design feature was added after multiple reports of people, especially children, choking on pen caps.

Pen manufacturers like BIC were among the first to incorporate this life-saving detail. Now, it's standard across many brands. So the next time you find yourself absentmindedly popping that cap in your mouth, remember, that little hole is there for a very important reason it could be the difference between a near-miss and a serious medical emergency.

Why Do Planes Dim the Lights During Takeoff and Landing?

It may seem like a small, routine procedure when the cabin lights dim just before takeoff or landing, but this action plays a critical role in aviation safety. Airlines dim the cabin lights to help your eyes adjust to low-light conditions, just in case an emergency evacuation is needed. Imagine this scenario: you're flying at night, and something goes wrong during takeoff or landing. If the plane's bright lights suddenly go out or you're thrust into darkness, your eyes would struggle to adjust quickly, leaving you disoriented.

Dimming the lights gradually brings your vision closer to the level of natural light outside, ensuring that, if you need to evacuate, your eyes are already acclimated. It can take anywhere from 10 to 30 minutes for your eyes to fully adjust to darkness, but dimming the lights for even a few minutes helps shorten this adjustment time. In an emergency, every second counts.

Additionally, dimming the lights makes the emergency floor lighting and exit signs easier to spot. In the rare event of a forced evacuation, these lights guide passengers to the nearest exits, even if visibility is compromised by smoke or other factors.

So the next time you're on a flight, remember that this small, seemingly insignificant action could make a world of difference if something goes wrong. It's a small but crucial aspect of aviation safety that's all about giving passengers the best possible chance to react quickly in an emergency.

Why Do Jeans Have Tiny Front Pockets?

Ever wonder about that tiny pocket inside your front jean pocket—the one that seems too small to hold anything useful? While it might seem like a quirky design feature, its origin is deeply rooted in practicality. That little pocket was originally designed to hold a pocket watch. Back in the 19th century, when Levi Strauss first created jeans for workers, many men carried pocket watches, which were essential for keeping time in industries like railroads, mining, and ranching.

Before wristwatches became popular, pocket watches were the primary timekeeping tool, especially for working men. The small pocket

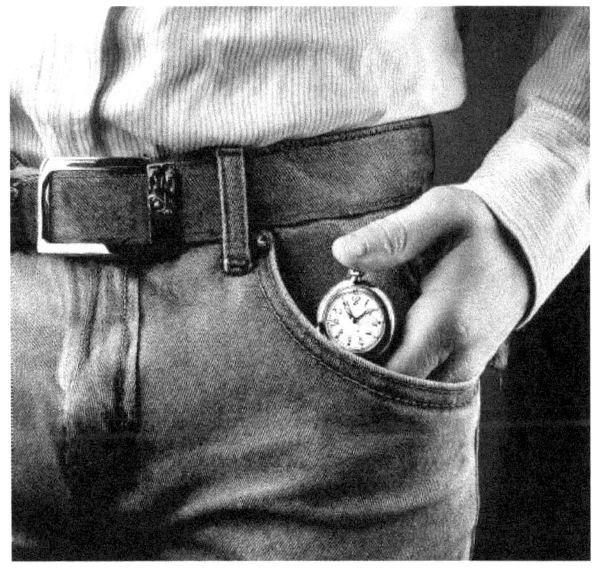

provided a safe, secure place to store the watch, preventing it from swinging or getting damaged while working. The design was such a hit that it became a standard feature of jeans, and even though pocket watches are long out of style, the pocket has stuck around.

Today, the pocket has taken on new uses. People stash all kinds of small items in there—coins, guitar picks, lighters, or even earbuds. Despite being a relic of the past, it remains an iconic part of jean design, representing the rich history of workwear and the transition from utility to fashion.

What's the Purpose of the Extra Shoelace Holes at the Top of Running Shoes?

Runners often ignore the extra shoelace holes at the top of their shoes, but these tiny eyelets hold the secret to preventing blisters and providing more ankle support. They're part of a clever design feature known as the heel lock, a technique that secures your foot in place and reduces uncomfortable slipping during activity.

Here's why it matters: when you're running or hiking, your feet tend to slide forward inside your shoes, causing friction. This friction can lead to blisters, especially during long distances. The extra holes are there to help you create a snug fit around the ankle without tightening

the whole shoe. By threading your laces through these top holes, you create a loop that locks your heel in place, preventing unnecessary movement.

What's fascinating is that this simple trick has been used by athletes for decades, but many casual runners never realize its potential. The next time you lace up your running shoes, give the heel lock a try—it might just save you from pain and discomfort during your next workout. It's a perfect example of how a small design detail can make a big difference in your performance. its potential. The next time you lace up your running shoes, give the heel lock a try—it might just save you from pain and discomfort during your next workout. It's a perfect example of how a small design detail can make a big difference in your performance.

What Do the Numbers on Plastic Items Mean?

The numbers inside the recycling triangle on plastic items are far more than just a symbol—they are the key to understanding the complex world of plastic recycling. Each number, from 1 to 7, refers to a specific type of plastic, and knowing these distinctions can help you make more environmentally conscious decisions.

• #1 PET (Polyethylene Terephthalate): This is the most common type of plastic, used in water bottles, soda bottles, and food packaging.

It's widely recycled, often turned into new bottles, clothing, or carpeting. However, PET breaks down with repeated use, meaning it's best recycled after one or two uses.

• #2 HDPE (High-Density Polyethylene): Found in milk jugs, detergent bottles, and grocery bags, HDPE is durable and has a low risk of leaching harmful chemicals. It's commonly recycled into more bottles, piping, or plastic lumber.

• #3 PVC (Polyvinyl Chloride): Used for plumbing pipes,

medical equipment, and some packaging, **PVC** is difficult to recycle and can release harmful toxins when burned, making it one of the least eco-friendly plastics.

• **#4 LDPE (Low-Density Polyethylene):** You'll find this in plastic wrap, grocery bags, and squeezable bottles. While less commonly recycled, there's a growing movement to recycle more LDPE due to its flexibility and durability.

• **#5 PP (Polypropylene):** This strong, heat-resistant plastic is used in yogurt containers, bottle caps, and takeout containers. It's increasingly accepted at recycling facilities and is often repurposed into signal lights, battery cables, and even synthetic carpets.

• **#6 PS (Polystyrene):** Commonly known as Styrofoam, this plastic is difficult to recycle and often ends up in landfills or as ocean debris. It's used in disposable cups, takeout boxes, and packing materials.

• **#7 Other:** This catch-all category includes polycarbonate, used in electronics and some baby bottles, and bioplastics, which are often biodegradable.

Understanding these numbers helps you become a more informed recycler and advocate for better recycling practices. It can guide your purchases and disposal methods, reducing the impact of plastic waste on the environment.

Why Are Pencils Traditionally Yellow?

The color of a pencil may seem like a mundane detail, but its yellow hue is a nod to luxury and prestige from a bygone era. In the late 1800s, the finest graphite came from China, and European pencil makers wanted to advertise that their pencils contained this top-tier material. But how could they stand out in a crowded market?

Enter the yellow pencil. Yellow was a color associated with Chinese royalty, symbolizing respect, wisdom, and power. The Czech pencil manufacturer Koh-I-Noor was the first to paint its pencils yellow to signal the high quality of the Chinese graphite inside. The yellow pencils were a hit at the 1889 World's Fair, and soon, other manufacturers followed suit. What started as a marketing strategy evolved into a global standard for pencil color.

Today, even though pencils no longer rely on Chinese graphite, the yellow pencil remains a cultural icon. It's a familiar tool that evokes the history of international trade, marketing genius, and even royalty—all in one humble writing instrument.

The Easiest Way to Peel a Banana

Most people peel a banana from the stem end, where it naturally curves, but there's an easier way that minimizes the risk of bruising or smashing the banana. The trick? Peel it like a monkey!

HERE'S HOW:

1. Pinch the bottom of the banana (the opposite end from the stem).
2. You'll see the skin split open effortlessly.
3. Once split, peel back the skin from the base, and your banana is ready to eat.

WHY IS THIS BETTER?

- Less pressure on the banana: Peeling from the stem can sometimes squish the fruit. Pinching the bottom is gentler, preventing bruising or squishing.
- Easier grip: The stem end is left intact, giving you a natural handle for holding the banana as you eat.

This method is commonly used by monkeys, and it's surprisingly efficient!

Why Do Airplane Windows Have Tiny Holes?

If you've ever looked closely at the windows on an airplane, you may have noticed a small hole at the bottom of each windowpane. This tiny feature is known as a breather hole or bleed hole, and it plays a crucial role in maintaining the safety and comfort of passengers at high altitudes.

Pressure Regulation
At cruising altitude, the air pressure inside the cabin is significantly higher than the pressure outside the plane. Airplane windows are typically made of three layers: the outer pane, which is the strongest and bears the pressure difference between the inside and outside of the plane, the middle pane, and the inner pane closest to the passengers.

The tiny hole is located in the middle pane and serves to regulate the pressure between the inner and outer layers of the window. It allows air from the cabin to equalize the pressure between the cabin and the space between the panes, which reduces the stress on the outer pane. Essentially, the outer pane takes the full pressure load, while the middle and inner panes provide backup.

Preventing Fogging
In addition to pressure regulation, the tiny hole also helps to prevent fogging or frost from forming on the window. The hole allows moist air trapped between the panes to escape, ensuring that the window stays clear, so passengers can enjoy the view without condensation buildup.

Safety Feature
In the unlikely event that the outer pane fails, the middle and

inner panes are designed to act as a safety buffer. The tiny hole helps maintain the integrity of the window by ensuring that the outer pane bears most of the pressure, keeping passengers safe and comfortable.

Why Does Food Taste Different on Airplanes?

If you've ever wondered why airline food often seems bland or less flavorful, it's not necessarily because of the quality of the meal. Instead, the unique conditions inside an airplane cabin affect your taste buds and sense of smell, making food taste different at high altitudes.

Reduced Sensitivity to Taste
At cruising altitude, the cabin is pressurized, but the air inside is still much drier and the pressure is lower than at ground level. The low humidity (typically around 12%) and lower pressure cause your mucous membranes to dry out, which dulls your sense of smell—an important component of tasting food. Since 80% of taste is actually smell, when your ability to smell is reduced, food can taste less flavorful.

The changes in pressure also affect your taste buds directly. Studies show that at high altitudes, your sensitivity to sweet and salty flavors decreases by around 30%. This is why airline food is often seasoned more heavily than normal food to make up for the diminished taste perception. Spicy and savory (umami) flavors tend to hold up better in the dry cabin air, which is why you might notice stronger seasoning in certain airline meals.

Noise and Taste Perception
Another surprising factor that affects how food tastes in the air is the level of background noise. Airplane cabins are typically filled with a constant hum of engines and airflow, which has been shown to further reduce your ability to taste. Studies suggest that the loud environment

can dull sweet and salty flavors while enhancing umami (savory) tastes. This is why foods like tomato juice are popular choices on flights—it has a strong umami flavor that stands out in the noisy cabin.

Altering Menus to Compensate
To combat the effects of dry air, low pressure, and noise, airlines often adjust their menus by choosing dishes that are naturally flavorful and umami-rich, such as curries, stews, or foods with strong seasonings. They also often add more salt and spices to meals to make the flavors pop. Some airlines have even worked with top chefs and food scientists to develop in-flight menus specifically designed to taste good under the unique conditions of air travel.

In summary, it's not just your imagination—your food really does taste different when you're flying. The combination of dry air, low pressure, and constant noise alters your perception of flavors, making airline meals less flavorful than they would be on the ground.

Why Does Coffee Make Some People Tired Instead of Energized?

For most people, coffee acts as a stimulant, helping them feel more awake and focused. However, some people experience the opposite effect, feeling tired or sluggish after drinking coffee. This unexpected reaction to caffeine can happen for a few reasons related to how your body processes the stimulant.

Caffeine and Adenosine
Caffeine works by blocking a neurotransmitter called adenosine in your brain. Adenosine is responsible for making you feel drowsy throughout the day, building up in your brain as you get closer to bedtime. When you drink coffee, caffeine temporarily blocks the adenosine receptors, making you feel more alert.

However, as the caffeine wears off, your body's adenosine continues to accumulate. For some people, when the caffeine starts to leave the system, the adenosine surge can feel even stronger, causing them to feel more tired than before. It's like your brain is making up for lost time, hitting you with a wave of fatigue once the effects of the caffeine diminish.

The Caffeine Crash
Another reason coffee can make you feel tired is the infamous caffeine crash. While caffeine provides an initial energy boost, it also triggers a spike in blood sugar levels and increases the production of stress hormones like adrenaline. After this spike, you can
To minimize the chance of feeling tired after coffee:

experience a sudden drop in blood sugar, leaving you feeling tired, irritable, and sometimes shaky. This "crash" can be particularly noticeable in people who are sensitive to caffeine or if they've consumed too much at once.

Individual Sensitivity to Caffeine

Not everyone processes caffeine the same way. Some people are naturally more sensitive to caffeine due to genetic differences in how they metabolize it. These individuals may break down caffeine more slowly, causing it to linger in their system longer. Instead of experiencing a steady boost of energy, the prolonged effects of caffeine can overwhelm their system, leading to feelings of exhaustion rather than alertness.

Coffee and Dehydration

Coffee is a diuretic, which means it increases the amount of urine you produce. For some people, this effect can lead to mild dehydration if they don't drink enough water alongside their coffee. Dehydration can contribute to fatigue, so if you feel tired after drinking coffee, it could be because your body is lacking fluids.

Anxiety and Overstimulation

For those who are sensitive to caffeine, coffee can sometimes overstimulate the body, leading to feelings of anxiety, jitteriness, or heart palpitations. This stress response can leave you feeling mentally and physically drained, leading to a sensation of tiredness even while your body is in a heightened state of alertness.

How to Avoid Feeling Tired After Coffee

Drink plenty of water: Stay hydrated to counteract the diuretic effects of caffeine.

Don't overdo it: Stick to moderate amounts of caffeine, as large doses are more likely to lead to a crash.

Pair coffee with food: Eating a small meal or snack with your coffee can help maintain stable blood sugar levels and prevent the crash that comes with a caffeine high.

In summary, while caffeine can be a great pick-me-up for many, factors like adenosine buildup, caffeine sensitivity, and even dehydration can leave some people feeling more tired after drinking coffee. Understanding how your body reacts to caffeine can help you enjoy coffee without the unintended side effects.

Why Does Aluminum Foil Have a Shiny Side and a Dull Side?

If you've ever noticed that aluminum foil has one side that's shiny and another side that's dull, you may have wondered if there's any difference between the two when it comes to cooking or storing food. The truth is, the shiny and dull sides are a result of the manufacturing process, and for most uses, they are functionally identical.

The Manufacturing Process
Aluminum foil is created by rolling large sheets of aluminum into progressively thinner layers. As it gets thinner, manufacturers run two layers of foil through a set of rollers at the same time. The side of the foil that is in contact with the highly polished rollers ends up shiny, while the side that touches the other sheet of aluminum remains dull. This process allows manufacturers to produce the extremely thin sheets of foil that are commonly used in kitchens.

Is There a Difference in Cooking?
Many people believe that the shiny side reflects heat while the dull side absorbs it, leading to different cooking results. However, in most cases, this is a myth. When it comes to heat conduction in cooking, there is no significant difference between the shiny and dull sides of aluminum foil. Both sides conduct heat equally well and will not affect the cooking or baking process.

There is one exception: If you're using aluminum foil in conjunction with heat-sensitive tasks, like freezing or when using a specific type of insulation for heat-sensitive foods, the shiny side may help reflect light and retain temperature more effectively. However, for everyday cooking tasks such as covering a baking dish or wrapping food, the difference between the two sides is negligible.

When Does It Matter?
In rare cases, recipes may specify using one side of the foil over the other for presentation purposes. For instance, if you're serving food wrapped in foil at a formal event, you might prefer the shiny side for aesthetic reasons. Aside from that, the decision to use the shiny or dull side is entirely a matter of personal preference.

In summary, the shiny and dull sides of aluminum foil are simply a byproduct of how the foil is made, and they function the same in most cooking situations. Next time you use aluminum foil, feel free to choose whichever side you like—both are equally effective!

Why Do Some People Get Brain Freeze?

We've all been there—taking a big bite of ice cream or sipping a cold drink on a hot day, only to feel a sudden, sharp pain in our head that makes us wince. This phenomenon, commonly known as brain freeze or an ice cream headache, is a short-lived but uncomfortable experience. But why does it happen, and what causes that intense burst of pain?

What Causes Brain Freeze?
Brain freeze happens when something cold (like ice cream, slushies, or cold drinks) touches the roof of your mouth, or the hard palate. When the cold substance hits this sensitive area, it triggers a series of reactions in the blood vessels inside your mouth. The cold causes the blood vessels in the roof of your mouth to constrict (tighten) and then rapidly dilate (widen) as they try to warm the area back up. This sudden change in the size of the blood vessels leads to increased blood flow, and the nerves in the region send pain signals to the brain.

The key player in this process is the trigeminal nerve, which is responsible for sensing pain in your face, mouth, and throat. When this nerve detects the sudden temperature change, it sends signals to your brain, which interprets the sensation as pain coming from your forehead rather than your mouth. This phenomenon is called referred pain, meaning that the pain is felt in a location other than where it originates.

Why the Intensity?
Brain freeze pain feels so intense because the trigeminal nerve is very sensitive and closely linked to both your face and your brain's pain pathways. The sudden spike in blood flow during the dilation phase

causes a quick, intense burst of pain, which usually lasts no more than 30 seconds to a minute. As soon as the blood vessels return to their normal state, the pain subsides.

Does Everyone Get Brain Freeze?
Interestingly, not everyone experiences brain freeze, and it seems to be more common in people who experience migraines. Some researchers believe this is because people who suffer from migraines have a more sensitive trigeminal nerve, making them more prone to this type of referred pain.

How to Avoid Brain Freeze
To prevent brain freeze, try warming the roof of your mouth after taking a bite of something cold. You can do this by pressing your tongue against the roof of your mouth, or by drinking something warm to balance out the cold sensation. Eating or drinking cold foods slowly can also help prevent the rapid temperature change that triggers brain freeze.

In summary, brain freeze is your body's way of reacting to a sudden and extreme cold stimulus, resulting in a short but intense headache. While it can be uncomfortable, it's generally harmless and easy to avoid by taking your time with cold foods.

Why Do Your Fingers Wrinkle in Water?

When you spend time soaking in a bath, swimming, or doing the dishes, you've likely noticed your fingers and toes become wrinkled. For a long time, scientists believed this wrinkling was a result of the skin absorbing water, causing it to swell and buckle. However, more recent research has shown that this isn't simply a passive process but rather an active reaction controlled by your nervous system.

THE ROLE OF THE NERVOUS SYSTEM

The wrinkling of your fingers and toes in water is actually caused by the autonomic nervous system, the part of your body that controls involuntary actions such as heart rate and breathing. When your fingers are submerged in water, particularly cool water, your body sends a signal that causes the blood vessels in your fingers to constrict, which reduces the volume of the soft tissues in your fingertips. As a result, the skin above the blood vessels collapses into folds, creating the characteristic wrinkling pattern.

This reaction is driven by the sympathetic nervous system, the same system that's responsible for the fight-or-flight response. This means that wrinkling in water is not just a side effect of being submerged, but an evolutionary adaptation.

WHY DOES IT HAPPEN?

Researchers now believe that finger and toe wrinkling in water serves an important functional purpose: it improves grip. The wrinkled skin acts like the tread on tires, giving you a better hold on wet, slippery objects. This would have been particularly useful for our ancestors, who often needed to gather food or use tools in wet environments.

Wrinkled fingers may have helped early humans get a better grip on wet plants, tools, or slippery fish.

In fact, studies have shown that people with wrinkled fingers are able to grip wet objects more effectively than those with smooth, unwrinkled fingers. This suggests that the wrinkling response may have evolved to help humans navigate or manipulate objects in aquatic environments.

WHY ONLY FINGERS AND TOES?

Wrinkling happens on fingers and toes because these areas have a high concentration of nerve endings and blood vessels, which allows the autonomic nervous system to control them more effectively. Other parts of your body don't wrinkle in the same way because the skin in those areas doesn't have the same level of vascular control or need for enhancement.

WHAT IF YOUR FINGERS DON'T WRINKLE?

Interestingly, if your fingers don't wrinkle after prolonged exposure to water, it could indicate an issue with the nervous system, such as nerve damage or a problem with blood flow. Medical professionals sometimes use the absence of finger wrinkling as a diagnostic tool for assessing nerve function.

In summary, finger wrinkling in water is a nervous system response that likely evolved to enhance our grip in wet conditions. Far from being an incidental side effect of water exposure, this reaction serves a purpose that may have helped our ancestors survive in wet environments.

Why Do We Get Goosebumps?

Goosebumps are a physical reaction that occurs when tiny muscles at the base of hair follicles contract, causing the hair to stand up. This reaction, known as piloerection, is a remnant of an ancient reflex shared with many other mammals. It can be triggered by several stimuli, including cold temperatures, strong emotions like fear or excitement, or even certain medical conditions.

EVOLUTIONARY ORIGINS

Goosebumps are part of our body's fight-or-flight response, controlled by the sympathetic nervous system. This system kicks into action when you experience stress, fear, or cold, releasing adrenaline. In animals, particularly those with thick fur, goosebumps serve two important functions:

1. Thermoregulation: When the hair stands up, it traps a layer of air close to the skin, creating insulation and helping the animal stay warm.

2. Self-defense: Goosebumps make an animal's fur stand on end, making them look bigger and more intimidating to predators. Think of a cat puffing up its fur when it feels threatened.

In humans, however, this reflex has become largely obsolete. Our body hair is so fine that goosebumps don't offer the same insulation or protective advantage as they do in fur-covered animals. Yet, we still experience the same reflex because it's hardwired into our nervous system.

EMOTIONAL TRIGGERS

Goosebumps aren't just caused by cold—they're also closely tied to emotions. Strong emotional experiences, such as fear, awe, nostalgia, or even listening to music, can trigger goosebumps. This happens because the amygdala, the part of the brain that processes emotions, also plays a role in activating the fight-or-flight response. When we feel deeply moved or startled, the same adrenaline that helps us deal with physical danger can also cause the piloerection response.

This emotional goosebump reaction is often referred to as "frisson"— the chills you get when you hear a powerful piece of music, watch an emotional scene in a movie, or experience something awe-inspiring. Studies suggest that this is part of the brain's way of processing intense or moving experiences, providing both a physical and emotional response.

MEDICAL CONDITIONS

Sometimes, goosebumps can occur without any apparent trigger. In certain medical conditions, such as fever, panic attacks, or even neurological disorders, the sympathetic nervous system can be overactive, causing goosebumps to appear in unusual situations. This response can also occur in the context of cold-induced sweating or other conditions where the nervous system is overstimulated.

SUMMARY

While goosebumps no longer serve a crucial role for modern humans, they are a fascinating leftover from our evolutionary past. Whether triggered by cold temperatures or strong emotions, they provide a glimpse into the way our bodies are wired to react to the world around us—both physically and emotionally.

Why Do You Sometimes Hear the Ocean in a Seashell?

You've probably heard that familiar whooshing sound when you hold a seashell up to your ear, and many people believe that this sound is the ocean. However, the truth is a bit more interesting: the sound you hear has nothing to do with the ocean, and everything to do with sound waves and resonance.

The Physics of Sound Waves
When you hold a seashell up to your ear, what you're actually hearing is the amplification of ambient noise in the environment around you. Seashells act like natural resonators or echo chambers—they capture and amplify the sounds that are already present, such as the air moving around, distant voices, or your own blood circulating through your body.

The shape of the seashell creates a resonating cavity that filters and amplifies certain sound frequencies, making them sound like the rush of ocean waves. Essentially, the shell's curved shape bounces and reverberates sound waves inside it, creating the illusion of the ocean. The result is a whooshing sound that mimics the sound of waves crashing.

Does It Have to Be a Seashell?
Interestingly, the seashell itself isn't required for this effect to happen. You can achieve the same sound with other hollow objects, like a cup, a glass, or even your cupped hands held tightly over your ears. As long as there's a cavity for the sound waves to bounce around in, you'll hear

that same rushing noise. The seashell just happens to be a commonly found, naturally shaped object that works well for this purpose.

AMBIENT NOISE AND ITS ROLE

The sound you hear will be influenced by the level of ambient noise around you. If you're in a noisy environment, the whooshing sound will be louder because there are more sound waves for the shell to pick up and amplify. Conversely, in a very quiet room, the sound will be much fainter, but you might hear the blood flow in your own ears more  distinctly, as the shell amplifies that subtle internal noise.

THE ROLE OF AIR PRESSURE

Another factor contributing to the sound is air pressure. The air inside the shell (or any other object you use) is trapped and disturbed by the movement of sound waves, which then bounce around the shell's hollow interior. This movement creates the familiar sound we associate with the ocean, even though it's just the result of air and sound waves interacting within the shell.

SUMMARY

So, while it's fun to think you're hearing the distant ocean, the reality is that the seashell is simply amplifying the sounds around you, creating an echo-like effect that mimics the sound of waves. Whether it's the movement of air, external noise, or even the blood rushing through your own body, the seashell works like a mini acoustic chamber, allowing you to hear the "ocean" wherever you are.

Why Do Some People Sneeze When They Look at Bright Lights?

The phenomenon where people sneeze after looking at bright lights, such as the sun or a bright bulb, is called the photic sneeze reflex, or more scientifically, autosomal dominant compelling helio-ophthalmic outburst syndrome (ACHOO). This quirky reaction is more common than you might think, affecting around 18-35% of the population. But what exactly causes it?

Crossed Wiring in the Brain
The leading theory is that the photic sneeze reflex is caused by crossed wiring in the brain. The trigeminal nerve, which controls sneezing, and the optic nerve, which detects light, are located near each other in the brain. In individuals with this reflex, the signals from the optic nerve—triggered by bright light—"spill over" and stimulate the trigeminal nerve, which then sends a signal to the body to sneeze. Essentially, the brain is misinterpreting the light stimulus as a need to sneeze.

A Genetic Trait
The photic sneeze reflex is believed to be genetic, passed down through families in an autosomal dominant pattern, meaning that if one parent has the reflex, their child has a 50% chance of inheriting it. This is why some people are more prone to sneezing when exposed to bright lights, while others are unaffected.

Evolutionary Purpose?
While it may seem like an odd quirk, some researchers speculate that there could have been an evolutionary advantage to the photic sneeze nasal passages when emerging from dark caves or shelters. However,

this is more of a hypothesis, as the reflex doesn't serve a clear biological purpose today.

How It Works
Here's how the process generally plays out:

Exposure to Bright Light: When someone with the photic sneeze reflex steps into bright sunlight or looks directly at a bright artificial light, their optic nerve is stimulated.
Crossed Signals: The stimulus intended for the optic nerve spills over and activates the trigeminal nerve, which is responsible for facial sensations, including the reflex to sneeze.
Sneezing Response: The trigeminal nerve then mistakenly signals the brain that there's a need to sneeze, causing the person to experience the familiar involuntary reaction of sneezing.
Variability in Sensitivity
Not everyone experiences the same intensity of the reflex. For some, even a brief glimpse of sunlight can trigger a sneezing fit, while for others, it may take prolonged exposure to a bright light source. Interestingly, the number of sneezes can vary too—some people sneeze just once, while others may sneeze multiple times in rapid succession.

Managing the Reflex
There's no way to "cure" the photic sneeze reflex, but people who experience it can try a few techniques to minimize the effect:

Wearing sunglasses: This can help block the intensity of bright sunlight, reducing the likelihood of sneezing.
Gradually exposing the eyes to bright light: Giving your eyes time to adjust to the brightness may reduce the trigger for sneezing.

Looking away from direct light sources can also help avoid the reflex. In summary, the photic sneeze reflex is a curious genetic trait likely caused by crossed signals between the optic and trigeminal nerves. It's harmless but can catch people off guard when they encounter sudden bright light. While not everyone experiences it, those who do have likely inherited it from their parents.